HA
THI

Ghost Stories

Prepare to be frightened by these terrifying tales from
around Hampshire and the Isle of Wight

BRADWELL
BOOKS

Published by Bradwell Books
9 Orgreave Close Sheffield S13 9NP
Email: books@bradwellbooks.co.uk

British Library Cataloguing in Publication Data: a catalogue
record for this book is available from the British Library.

1st Edition
ISBN: 9781909914476

Print: Gomer Press, Llandysul, Ceredigion SA44 4JL
Design by: jenksdesign@yahoo.co.uk
Photograph Credits:
iStock, Shutterstock and the author

CONTENTS

INTRODUCTION

Hampshire is a county of many parts. Its most populated area is situated along the south coast and includes the cities of Southampton and Portsmouth. To the west is the distinct area which has been known as the New Forest since the days of William the Conqueror. The New Forest consists of a few scattered villages and small towns in an otherwise unspoiled area of heath and woodland. The entire region is now a National Park. The Isle of Wight also belongs to Hampshire but forms, of course, a distinct region of its own, full of individual character. The remaining part of mainland Hampshire consists of pretty towns and villages in rolling countryside. Here can be found Winchester, Hampshire's county town and the former capital of England.

Hampshire is the birthplace of all the UK's Armed Forces: the Navy, Army and Air Force. But of them all, it is the Royal Navy and other maritime connections that have the most resonance. Southampton and Portsmouth are both important ports. A number of tourist attractions continue to celebrate Hampshire's maritime history and more than a few of them are haunted. These include several defensive forts, now in the care of English Heritage, and Admiral Lord Nelson's famous flagship, HMS *Victory*, which is in dry dock in Portsmouth.

Spectral sailors are a feature of the county's haunted landscape. However, in numbers of apparitions they are rivalled by ghosts dating from the English Civil War. Phantom Roundheads and Royalists still clash more than 300 years on. It's extraordinary how many ghost stories have their origins in those few desperate years of the 17th century. Many other spooks date from Hampshire's medieval past, especially in ancient Winchester and the remains of its noble castles. A good many of the county's stately homes are haunted and so too are other attractions open to the public. Even in the wilder open spaces, such as the New Forest, ghosts may be encountered.

Among Hampshire's 'celebrity' ghosts are the writers Jane Austen and Alfred, Lord Tennyson and members of Royalty, including William Rufus and Anne Boleyn.

Hampshire is a fascinating county of great beauty and is blessed with many interesting and historic places to visit. Its haunted heritage is equally fascinating and can be enjoyed in tandem with more orthodox days (or nights!) out. I have arranged the haunted locations in a handy gazetteer, so you can easily find those closest to you. I hope it will whet your appetite to seek out more!

HMS Victory at Portsmouth: Hampshire's naval past has contributed many ghostly legends.

ALTON

This handsome market town in East Hampshire is associated with two very different notables, both of whom are said to haunt the place. One of these is 'Sweet Fanny Adams'. If you thought 'sweet FA' was just a phrase, think again, for Fanny Adams was a real – and most unfortunate – little girl. One summer's day in August, 1867, nine-year-old Fanny was brutally murdered by a psychopath named Frederick Baker. Baker, who worked as a solicitor's clerk, hacked up the little girl's body in a field near her home and then added a note in his diary of such astonishing disregard that it reminds one of Hannibal Lecter: 'August 24, Saturday. Killed a young girl. It was fine and hot.' The case was a sensation and the wretch was duly hanged.

In the same year, Royal Navy sailors found that their rations had been changed: out was the traditional ship's biscuit; in was a rather disgusting tinned meat. Unimpressed with the change and infused with a grim sense of humour, the mariners declared that the unknown meat product was actually the potted remains of 'sweet Fanny Adams'. The phrase stuck, meaning initially anything not worth having, but soon becoming the more profane 'sweet FA' still in use today. It didn't take long before there were tales of the ghost of the murdered girl being seen in the field where she met her tragic end.

A much more famous denizen of Alton was the Elizabethan poet Edmund Spenser. The author of *The Faerie Queene* lived in a house in Amery Street, now converted into two cottages, whose Georgian frontages disguise their greater age. Spenser, still a young man, wrote some of his finest work in this house.

His spectral form is now said to be seen pottering down Amery Street and has been variously described as 'a little man with short hair dressed in Elizabethan garb' (Peter Underwood, in his *Ghosts of Hampshire and the Isle of Wight*) or 'dressed in dark clothes and a tall hat' (Rupert Matthews in his *Haunted Hampshire*, quoting an unnamed source). Matthews notes that the latter might actually be the apparition of an Edwardian gentleman who died in 1918, so there may be two ghosts in Amery Street.

Alton's grand Church of St Lawrence, which has parts dating back to Saxon times, also has a haunted reputation. The church became the centre of a decidedly unholy battle between Royalist and Parliamentarian supporters during the English Civil War. Royalist soldiers commanded by a Colonel Boles holed up in the sacred building, using it as a kind of makeshift fortress, while a Roundhead force laid siege to it outside. The musket-ball holes are still to be seen in the masonry. Several people who have been alone in the church have reported the strange sensation that the empty building is somehow crammed with jostling and fighting men. Others have heard pops and cracks, as of musket fire, and indecipherable shouts and yells emanating from the churchyard.

It would seem that the most haunted place in Alton, however, is the 15th-century Crown Hotel in the centre of town. Here was heard the muffled whining and scratching of some unseen dog, the origin of which was apparently explained during renovation work in the 1960s: the skeleton of a small dog was found in a cavity behind a fireplace. The hole had been sealed up behind panelling for centuries. When Rupert Matthews visited the hotel, he was told about two further ghosts. One is

Elizabethan poet Edmund Spenser spent much of his life in Alton and haunts the street past his former home. iStock

the obsessively tidy spirit of a maid who likes to check up on today's staff to make sure 'everything is left nice and tidy' in one of the bedrooms. The other, known as 'Patrick' for reasons long since forgotten, haunts a downstairs bar. 'Patrick' also likes to move things about and also enjoys interfering with the electrics – the lights unexpectedly went out in the bar during Matthews's visit!

ANDOVER

The old market town of Andover in the north of the county has a haunted inn. The venerable White Hart Hotel in Bridge Street dates back to 1617 and King Charles I is believed to have stayed here. A range of spooky activity has been reported from the White Hart. The most commonly seen ghost is that of a tall woman dressed in either a gown or long cloak of a dark green colour. She patrols one of the upper corridors and also manifests in Room 20. 'Vague shapes' have been glimpsed in several other rooms, including in the bar. One barman who witnessed this phenomenon said: 'It was as if a couple of people had literally drifted through. Not quite white, but semi-transparent. They had no definite outline but resembled a man and a woman.'

Phantom footsteps have also been heard on the stairs and along an upper floor corridor. On one occasion they pursued a maid, who had to lock herself in a room to avoid them.

BASINGSTOKE

By an odd coincidence, Basingstoke's haunted pub is also a White Hart Inn. The White Hart on London Road is haunted by a peculiar phenomenon that sounds like something heavy being rolled over gravel. One might think it's simply the sound of some beer barrel of the past being rolled to the cellar, but it occurs in one of the upstairs rooms. The noise has only ever been heard after midnight and in previous years has been annoyingly loud and continuous, preventing sleep. The invisible thing rolls heavily towards the hearer and then, just as it's about to reach him or her, rolls away again. What the sound represents has remained entirely obscure.

On just one occasion, the ghost of a man has been seen in the room, running his fingers through his hair and apparently regarding himself in a now missing mirror. Who he is or whether he has any connection with the weird sound also remain unknown.

The best-known haunted location in Basingstoke is Basing House. Properly speaking the house is in Old Basing, a satellite village of the modern town. Basing House was built from 1531 for the First Marquess of Winchester, William Paulet. In its day it was a grand palace, standing five storeys high and boasting a total of 380 rooms. Some historians consider that at the time Basing House was the finest private home in England. Today, however, it is a ruin, thanks to Oliver Cromwell. In the Civil War, the Fifth Marquess owned Basing House and he was a staunch Royalist. On two occasions Parliamentarian forces laid siege to the mansion, but were driven off. Finally, in August 1645, a new siege was implemented and it was joined by an even larger force under the command of Cromwell himself. Basing House was eventually stormed and the Fifth Marquess imprisoned in the Tower of London.

During the siege Basing House was largely destroyed by fire. Afterwards Cromwell ordered that what remained was to be torn down and the bricks and fine stonework sold off. This is the reason so little survives of it today. Nevertheless it is an attractive spot to visit. The ruins are in the heart of an old motte and bailey fortification. Excavations have revealed more of the house than was previously visible and interpretive signs have been set up.

Ghosts of the Royalist defenders of Basing House have been seen around the site. One of them is particularly noticeable,

What little is left of Basing House is haunted by ghosts from the days of the disastrous Civil War siege that destroyed it. Shutterstock/BasPhoto

for he is remarkably tall. Intriguingly, one of the excavations in the grounds uncovered a number of burials, including one which contained a skeleton well over six feet tall. Perhaps it belonged to the man whose ghost has since been seen.

A few miles north-east of Basingstoke, just before the hamlet of Sherfield-on-Loddon, can be found Sherfield School. The school is incorporated into a grand country house formerly known as Sherfield Manor. In Sir Ernest Bennett's classic work on the supernatural, *Apparitions and Haunted Houses*, published in 1939, he reproduces a first-hand sighting of a ghost at Sherfield Manor. The witness was personally known to him: a barrister by the name of Irene Copper-Willis. Ms Cooper-Willis was staying in the house in the summer of 1926. One night she woke up to see a stranger in her room. She writes:

'The bed was an old-fashioned four-poster and at the bottom, between the bed and the fireplace, was a settee with back and sides. I woke suddenly. Either there was a moon outside or it was very early morning for I could see faint light outside the window – the curtains weren't drawn, and I could see things in the room. I saw the figure of a woman sitting slightly sideways on the settee at the bottom of the bed, with her head in her hands. Her hair was dark and I saw a ring on the hand cupping her head. She had a grey dress on, as far as I could see, with big sleeves; I could not see her skirt for the back of the settee was higher than the bed.

'She sat there without moving and as I looked at her I felt frightened for though I sat bolt upright, she never moved. I remembered that I could not turn the bedside light on, and I was too frightened to get out and switch on the light from the door. It seemed to me that I sat upright looking at her for at least half an hour, but my heart was beating and it is quite likely that I exaggerated the time from my first sight of her and her sudden vanishing. Suddenly she wasn't there: that's all I can say and then I immediately got out of bed, switched on the light and lay with the light on in bed until I heard a clock outside strike five and saw the daylight was on the way. I then went to sleep again.'

Ms Cooper-Willis continued to sleep in the room for a few more nights but did not see the apparition again. Her hostess knew nothing of the ghost, but had not been living in the house for very long.

BEAULIEU

This delightful village in the New Forest is home to Lord and Lady Montagu, whose splendid home, Beaulieu Palace House, is open to the public. The house was originally built in the 13th century as the gatehouse to a mighty abbey founded during the reign of King John. Tradition has it John suffered a nightmare in which he was repeatedly flogged by monks and awoke to find that he was covered in bruises. He had recently imprisoned a number of Cistercian monks after a dispute over taxation and he was so alarmed by the dream that not only did he order their release, he also donated land at Beaulieu so that the Cistercian Order could build another abbey.

The shades of these medieval monks haunt the ruins of Beaulieu Abbey and the surrounding area. They have been seen on a good many occasions by numerous witnesses. Usually they are observed merely pottering about, singly or in groups, but there is one who appears in the cloisters, sitting in

There is much ghostly activity reported from Beaulieu Palace House (top) and the ruins of Beaulieu Abbey, the entrance to which can be seen just beyond the parish church (bottom picture).
Shutterstock Dave/Greenberg (top) Shutterstock/Geno EJ Sajko (bottom)

a recess and reading a scroll. The actress Margaret Rutherford was one of those who claimed to have seen this latter ghost. In addition to the sightings of monks, they have also been heard chanting among the ruins. Behind the parish church, where the old monks' burial ground lay, shuffling footsteps have been heard, as if a funeral procession was taking place. The heady aroma of incense can unexpectedly spring up in the abbey and has also been detected in a dining room in Beaulieu Palace House.

The Palace House is also said to be haunted by Countess Isabella Montagu. Dressed in a blue gown, her ghost patrols the private apartments and has also been spotted in the Abbey, making its way from the cloisters to the family vault.

BRADING (Isle of Wight)

Brading, on the east coast of the Isle of Wight, was an important port in past centuries. Its use dates back to before the time of the Roman occupation. It is thought that Quay Lane, which squeezes past the 800-year-old church down to the sea, may originally have been used by Phoenician merchants. Opposite the entrance to Quay Lane is one of the oldest domestic buildings on the island: Old Rectory Mansion, which began life in the early 13th century before being converted into a Tudor manor house in 1499.

By the 17th century, Old Rectory Mansion had been converted into the Crown Inn. A dramatic tale is told about the building during this time. At the end of the Civil War, while Charles I languished in Carisbrooke Castle, a prisoner of Parliament, a Frenchman named de Rochefort arrived by ship and put up at the Crown. During the night, someone crept into his room and murdered him in his bed, stabbing the poor man three or four times as he screamed in agony. There are conflicting theories as to the reason for his death. One argues that he may have been a spy with a message to bring to Charles and was assassinated before he could deliver it. Alternatively, he may have been an assassin himself, hired by Oliver Cromwell to kill the king. The killer was never caught.

The murdered Frenchman's ghost has haunted the Old Rectory Mansion ever since. He is said to have cursed his unknown killer and with his dying breath threatened to haunt the house unless his body was buried on French soil (this was not complied with). As Peter Underwood puts it in his *Ghosts of Hampshire and the Isle of Wight*:

'Generations of occupants followed one another and the haunt continued. For more than a century the house was owned by a family named Carlet; one after the other they told of strange noises, inexplicable manifestations, the occasional glimpse of a tall, aristocratic figure in one of the bedrooms overlooking Quay Lane. Screams shatter the quiet of the night, the clatter of an invisible coach rattles down the lane outside the house.'

In the 1960s, the pub closed and the building housed one of the Isle of Wight's most popular tourist attractions: the Osborn-Smith Wax Museum. During this period, another, much less gloomy, ghost was detected in one of the outbuildings. The building was then being used as a pottery studio, with living space above it. The potter regularly heard pattering footsteps that would run from a bedroom down to the studio. They sounded like the lightly tripping steps of a child and tended to manifest in the middle of the afternoon. The sound of a door opening and closing sometimes accompanied the footsteps.

The Wax Museum closed down some years ago and the mansion has been empty since 2010. There is hope that it will be back on the Isle's tourist trail before long

The former seaport of Brading nestles among the hills on the east coast of the Isle of Wight. One of the old town's oldest buildings is famously haunted.
Shutterstock/Mike Charl

BRAMSHILL

The hamlet of Bramshill has become synonymous with the College of Policing in Bramshill House. Bramshill House is a splendid Jacobean red-brick mansion currently used as a training centre for British and European police officers. However, at the time of writing, plans were afoot to relocate the college to avoid the high costs of running and looking after such an architecturally important building. Perhaps one day it will be open to the public.

Bramshill House is claimed to be the original setting of a traditional English folk tale. Once upon a time, it was the custom for young brides to be 'kidnapped' by the groom's friends and carried off to the church. The girl was expected to put up at least a show of resistance, as a display of modesty. She would do this by playing hide and seek until the boisterous youths uncovered her, among much mirth. In this ghastly old yarn, however, hilarity turns to tragedy when the bride-to-be decides to hide inside an oak chest fitted with a spring lock. The heavy lid closes, trapping her inside. No one hears the poor girl's cries for help and she suffocates inside her premature coffin. It is many years before her corpse is found.

The Georgian poet Thomas Haynes Bayly popularised the legend in his poem 'The Mistletoe Bough':

> At length an old oak chest that had long laid hid
> Was found in the castle – they raised the lid;
> A skeleton form lay mouldering there,
> In the bridal wreath of that lady fair.
> Oh! Sad was her fate! In sportive jest
> She hid from her lord in that old oak chest.

It closed with a spring, and her bridal bloom
Lay withering there in a living tomb.

In Bayly's poem, the wedding was to have taken place over the Christmas season and the corpse is seen to still be clutching a sprig of mistletoe, given to her by her future husband. An elaborately carved chest in the entrance hall of Bramshill Hall is pointed out to visitors as the 'Mistletoe Bough Chest', in which the young woman had met her horrible end. The unfortunate bride is said to have haunted the house ever since her body was discovered. She is described as a fair maiden in a white gown who runs through the house on moonlit nights. She has sometimes been seen in the garden, too.

The White Lady is just one of many ghosts reported from Bramshill House, however. There is also a Grey Lady, who is thought to have been a member of the Copes, the family who owned Bramshill for centuries. Her main haunt is the Pale Pond, where, it is thought, she may have drowned, but she also turns up in the house. Described as 'a beautiful woman with lovely golden hair and wearing a grey dress', she is always accompanied by the scent of lilies. Another female figure has been seen leaping from a balustrade. Her identity is unknown but she is presumably the ghost of a suicide. In addition, a woman dressed in the style of the reign of Charles I haunts a bedroom and another in the fashions of Queen Anne has appeared in the Chapel Drawing Room.

One of the more unusual ghosts is the apparition of a man dressed entirely in green. He is thought to be of a Cope ancestor with a strange colour obsession. As well as wearing exclusively green garments, he painted his rooms and furniture the same colour and would only dine on green fruit and vegetables. This eccentric gentleman jumped off a Sussex cliff in 1806 and drowned in the sea (whether the sea was blue or green that day is not recorded, however!). A further apparition, that of a youth dressed as if ready to play a game of tennis, may be of a young Cope who died in 1930 when he fell from a train. The identities of the ghostly knight in armour seen in the Chapel Drawing Room and the long-bearded old man who peers in at a hall window remain unknown.

There are further spooks in the grounds of Bramshill House. The Keeper's Oak – a handsome old tree – is haunted by a gamekeeper of the 17th century who was killed when a clumsy archbishop mistook him for a deer while out hunting and launched an arrow at him. In addition, a mysterious figure has been seen on the old bridge over the river.

The remarkably haunted Bramshill House, sketched by Charles Harper for his 1930 book Mansions of Old Romance.

BUCKLER'S HARD

Buckler's Hard is a remarkable place. Located beside the meandering River Beaulieu, the hamlet was created in the 18th century by Lord Montagu as a handy port to facilitate his business interests in the West Indies. It soon became apparent that the port was little more than a folly, and Montagu Town, as it was then known, was taken over by the Royal Navy and used instead as a shipbuilding centre. It was here, at the renamed Buckler's Hard, that many of the ships which took part in the Battle of Trafalgar were constructed. Two centuries later, during the Second World War, Buckler's Hard was the gathering place for hundreds of small craft prior to the Normandy landings.

Buckler's Hard is one of Hampshire's most attractive haunted locations.
Shutterstock/Stanth

Today Buckler's Hard is a tourist attraction, a very pretty spot with a fascinating Maritime Museum on site. Echoes of the past are everywhere here but the ghost of Buckler's Hard is neither of a shipbuilder nor a seaman. It is of a small boy and he haunts the only modern building in the hamlet: the museum. Has he been somehow 'imported' along with one of the old artefacts on display? The spooky little fellow has been glimpsed on numerous occasions by staff and visitors alike; but who he is, nobody knows.

CHAWTON

This charming village is situated just a mile from Alton (see above) and is best known as being the former home of Jane Austen. Austen remains one of the world's most popular novelists, nearly 200 years after her early death in 1817 at the age of 41. Her insight into human nature combined with an ahead-of-its-time wit and wry look at social conventions has assured the lasting success of novels such as *Emma* and *Pride and Prejudice*.

Jane Austen spent her last eight years in a pleasing red-brick house in the middle of the village. She wrote all her novels in what is now Jane Austen's House Museum. The house has been restored to accurately represent a middle-class home of the early 19th century and contains many important 'Janeite' relics, including Austen's writing desk and a number of her handwritten manuscripts.

For years there have been rumours of Jane Austen's spirit lingering on in her former home. A member of the museum staff reported hearing an odd noise which drew her out into the garden to investigate. The garden was empty. As she stepped back into the house, however, she heard a disembodied female voice whisper 'Cass!' Had the ghost of Jane Austen mistaken the member of staff for her beloved sister Cassandra? In addition, footfalls have been detected in empty rooms and corridors and doors have the unnerving habit of opening and closing on their own at Jane Austen's House Museum.

Opposite the museum stands the Greyfriar pub, where the indistinct phantom of a woman manifests from time to time. Inevitably, it has been linked with Jane Austen (not much of a boozer, I'd have thought!) but there is even less reason to connect this paranormal phenomenon with the novelist than the manifestations at her former home.

Spooky goings-on have been reported from Jane Austen's former home in the village of Chawton, but whether or not they have anything to do with the continued presence of the great novelist is open to conjecture. iStock

CRONDALL

Of this village, situated in the north of the county, Rupert Matthews writes: 'Over the years, I have heard more tales in and about this place than any other village in Hampshire.' Crondall was formerly the home of one of Hampshire's best-known haunted houses, Itchel Manor. Itchel Manor was possessed of a spectral coach-and-horses that would be heard thundering up the drive before stopping before the front door. It was never seen, but its invisible visits were fairly regular. So too were the mysterious noises which all too often disturbed the household after dark. They included bangs and crashes, raps and thumps, and quick, hurried footsteps sometimes accompanied by the cry of a child. Weirdest of all was the unmistakable baa-ing of a flock of sheep heard outside a bedroom window! Needless to say, no sheep were visible at the time.

The manor house was also believed to be haunted by a former owner, the bad-tempered Squire Bathurst. He is said to have murdered one of his servants in a flash of rage, and then hushed up the crime. Another tale has it that it was he who was murdered, by a servant fed up with his mean, miserly ways. Itchel Manor was demolished in the 1950s.

Very much still a feature of the village, though, is the 12th-century Church of St Mary. During the English Civil War, the church was temporarily used as a fortification by Parliamentarian troops, with defensive embankments built up around the churchyard. A fierce battle was fought both in and outside the church, with a Royalist commander shooting down Roundheads from the pulpit. Remnants of this skirmish can still be seen today in the form of bullet holes in the walls, and gashes in old woodwork caused by slashing sabres.

Less substantial reminders of this drama are the apparitions of Roundhead soldiers which have been reported from the churchyard. Most impressive is the man on horseback who rides up the tree-lined path from the church door. This may be the ghost of Sir William Waller, who led the company of Roundheads. Odd noises which have been likened to the bangs and pops of musket fire have also been detected by villagers from time to time.

FRESHWATER (Isle of Wight)

From 1853 until his death in 1892, the Poet Laureate Alfred, Lord Tennyson lived at Farringford House in Freshwater. He loved the place. Most days he would walk around the surrounding countryside, more often than not climbing up nearby High Down (since renamed Tennyson Down) to enjoy the views. He built a summerhouse in the extensive grounds and here, surrounded by nature, wrote *The Idylls of the King* among other celebrated works. Farringford House became a hotel after Tennyson's death but, at the time of writing, it is closed to the public while an extensive renovation programme takes place. It will reopen as a study centre in 2016. (Alas the summerhouse is long gone).

It's good to know that some ghosts haunt places where they have been happiest, rather than because of the usual reason of some tragedy having befallen them. This is the case with Alfred, Lord Tennyson, whose shade is said to still be seen at

Farringford House and, from time to time, in the many neighbouring beauty spots. Should you encounter him on one of his ghostly rambles, you cannot mistake him, with his long flowing beard, his green frock coat and broad-brimmed hat.

Overlooking Freshwater Bay is the remarkable Golden Hill Fort, a hexagonal barrack-block built to house military personnel in the 1850s. The Grade I listed building has now been converted into eighteen private homes, each with its own rooftop garden, making Golden Hill Fort truly unique. Although the old fort itself is private property, the surrounding land is open to the public and is managed as a country park. The 360-degree view from the hillside is spectacular.

One can't help wondering whether the new owners of the luxury homes created at Golden Hill Fort are at all troubled by any of the ghosts reported from the facility in days gone by. One of these, unsurprisingly, is of a sailor. He stands in a doorway, his arms folded, leaning against the door jamb, perfectly at his ease. One story given to explain his presence is that he is the ghost of a sailor hanged for treason, but there is no record of such an execution and it hardly seems to fit with his relaxed demeanour. In addition to the phantom matelot, the apparition of a soldier from the First World War has been seen at Golden Hill Fort. Disembodied footsteps have also been reported.

Alfred, Lord Tennyson's distinctive figure is said to still be seen in the vicinity of his beloved home, Farringford House, at Freshwater.

GOSPORT

In common with Golden Hill Fort (see Freshwater, above), Fort Brockhurst, near Gosport, is part of a chain of defences constructed during the 1850s and 1860s to protect the coastline of Britain from possible attacks by the French. The forts were ordered to be built by the then Prime Minister Lord Palmerston and are therefore known as Palmerston Forts. In their day they were also known as Palmerston's Follies, because they cost so much and the feared invasion never came.

Fort Brockhurst was built to help protect the important naval base at Portsmouth. It is an impressive and well-preserved example, now in the care of English Heritage. As well as being an interesting place in its own right, the fort also houses a large display of diverse treasures from English Heritage's vast collection of artefacts. Should you visit, you might also hear the mysterious ghost, who is never seen but whose cheerful whistling has been heard wandering the passageways.

Nearby, on Stokes Bay, is another Palmerston Fort, Fort Gilkicker, once an extensive and heavily armed fortress but long since abandoned. Like Golden Hill Fort, there are plans to convert Fort Gilkicker into private apartments. Once completed, the occupants may possibly find themselves sharing their new homes with a ghost or two. David Scanlan has compiled quite a few sightings at Fort Gilkicker in his *Paranormal Hampshire*.

Scanlan spoke to security guards who had spooky experiences here. One told him that while he was watching CCTV feeds in his guardroom, he got the shivery feeling that he was being watched himself. He turned round and saw 'three spectral faces' pressed up against a window and peering in at him. He hurried outside but found the place deserted. The CCTV cameras had also failed to record the existence of the supposed intruders. Another spoke of encountering the shadowy figure of a man standing under one of the security lights. The guard demanded to know what he was doing there. The man turned to face him. 'Not a lot,' he replied – and vanished! The apparition of a little girl has also been seen in the old accommodation block.

Fort Brockhurst is one of several fortifications along the coast of Hampshire and the Isle of Wight with a haunted reputation. iStock

HIGHCLERE

Highclere Castle is a magnificent Jacobean mansion which has become world-famous as the stand-in for the titular *Downton Abbey* in Julian Fellowes's wildly successful 'posh soap'. The house is situated in the very north of the county, a few miles south of Newbury in Berkshire. It has been the seat of the Carnarvon family for centuries and is still the family home of Lord and Lady Carnarvon. However, much of the house is open to the public and crowds flock to experience the real-life 'Downton' for themselves. A less well-known attraction is that, according to Lady Carnarvon, Highclere Castle is haunted by three ghosts.

'We all know who they are,' Lady Carnarvon has told the Press. In an interview in *The Lady*, she said that the family's two pet Labradors are particularly sensitive to the ghosts' presence and she admitted to having seeing one of them herself.

'A few years ago, I saw one particular ghost, a footman, while I was with my young son Edward,' she explains. 'The older dog was on the other side of very heavy doors, and he went ballistic, barking crazily. He was as concerned and as worried as I was.'

Lady Carnarvon believes she knows the identity of the phantom. She continues: 'There was a footman here during the Victorian period, who committed suicide not far from where I'd seen him. He'd been having an affair with a nursemaid, who became pregnant. Sadly, their baby died, probably of cot death, and he killed himself. So there I was, a young countess with a new-born baby, and he came out. I was

Highclere Castle has at least three ghosts according to the current Lady of the manor. Shutterstock/Dutourdum

walking faster, and he was following, and then we decided to wish him all the best and send him on his way.

'Sometimes people get trapped – I just try to respect the people who've been here before.'

In an interview with *The Metro*, Lady Carnarvon added: 'A lot of people have lived here and I think you can tell when something terribly upsetting has happened in a room.'

One of the stars of *Downton Abbey*, the American actress Shirley MacLaine, mentioned in a separate interview that paintings had a habit of falling off the dining room walls during filming, but only when the spirits in the house 'didn't like the action'!

HINTON AMPNER

Hinton Ampner is a Georgian mansion with celebrated gardens near Alresford. It is a National Trust property. The current house replaced an earlier, Tudor mansion which was demolished in 1793. Earlier in that century, the now lost house became famously – or infamously – haunted.

Hinton Ampner was for centuries the home of the Stawell family. In 1740 the wife of the then Lord Stawell died and he made no secret of carrying on an affair with his sister-in-law, who had lived in the house for some time. The neighbourhood was scandalised, especially when rumour leaked out that a baby had been born: a baby that no one saw and which may have been done away with. One moonlit night shortly after Lord Stawell's own death in 1755, a groom announced that he had seen 'milord's' phantom wandering about in 'drab-coloured' (light brown) clothing.

In 1765 Hinton Ampner was rented out and the first family to take it were the Ricketts. It is from the testimony of Mrs Mary Ricketts, the lady of the house, that we learn of the ghosts. Initially, the haunting merely took the form of odd noises at night. Mr Ricketts spent many hours after dark, creeping about the passageways of Hinton Ampner in search of intruders he never found. On two occasions, servants were puzzled by seeing an unknown man in a drab-coloured coat about the house, but Mrs Ricketts dismissed these as 'the effect of fear or superstition to which the lower class of people are so prone' (!). Soon, however, the male figure was joined by a female one.

'In the month of July, 1767, about seven in the evening,' recorded Mrs Ricketts, 'the persons in the kitchen heard a woman come down-stairs, and along the passage leading towards them, whose clothes rustled as of the stiffest silk; and on their looking that way, the door standing open, a female figure rushed past, and out of the house door, as they conceived. Their view of her was imperfect; but they plainly distinguished a tall figure in dark-coloured clothes. Dame Brown, the cook, instantly coming in, the figure passed close by her, and instantly disappeared.'

When Mrs Ricketts began to hear repeatedly a sound resembling silk skirts rustling against the door leading into her bed-chamber, she began to realise the haunting was more than the superstition of the 'lower classes'. In 1769, Mr Ricketts left England to visit his estates in Jamaica. Almost immediately the disturbances became more intense but Mrs Ricketts refused to be scared out of her home. Over the following year, she heard heavy masculine footsteps walk into her bedroom on a number of occasions, on each occasion unaccompanied by anyone visible. She was also disturbed by loud knocks against a door and a 'hollow murmuring that seemed to possess the whole house'. On one occasion she was frightened by the sight of a door swinging back and forth as if someone was standing behind it. The room was found to be empty.

'After Midsummer,' writes Mrs Ricketts, 'the noises became every night more intolerable. They began before I went to bed, and with intermissions were heard till after broad day in the morning. I could frequently distinguish inarticulate sounds, and usually a shrill female voice would begin, and then two others with deeper and manlike tone seemed to join in the discourse; yet though this conversation sounded as if close to me, I never could distinguish words.'

On a subsequent night Mrs Ricketts and her servant, a certain Elizabeth Godin, heard 'the most loud, deep, tremendous noise, which seemed to rush and fall with infinite velocity and force on the lobby floor adjoining to my room'. Mrs Ricketts called out to Mrs Godin, but the latter was speechless with terror. To cap it off, both were then further alarmed by 'a shrill and dreadful shriek' emanating from the place where the rushing noise fell. Another servant, sleeping in a neighbouring room with the children, also heard the shriek. Since this was her first experience of the supernatural at Hinton Ampner, this woman found the experience more intriguing than frightening and rashly stated that she would be interested to hear more of the noises. From the night following, she was plagued by disturbances.

At last, Mrs Ricketts confided in her brother, a Captain John Jervis, of what was happening at Hinton Ampner. In response, he and a friend, Captain Luttrell, and a manservant, came to the house and, having made sure no one was hidden in the bedrooms or attic rooms, sat up all night to see what would happen. It did not take long for Captain Jervis and co. to discover the haunting was no fantasy. They heard footsteps, the rustling of silk and doors slamming, just as the womenfolk had. On subsequent nights they also heard a sound like a gunshot and bloodcurdling groans.

The result was that Jervis moved his sister and her family out of Hinton Ampner to live in a series of houses owned by various friends. In time another family, the Lawrences, moved into the house but they kept their cards close to their chest regarding any continuation of the haunting: they threatened their servants with instant dismissal if they blabbed about what was going on at Hinton Ampner. Nevertheless, word did get out of an apparition of a woman having been seen and other strange goings-on.

All in all, it's hardly surprising that the old Tudor manor house was shortly afterwards torn down and a brand new mansion built nearby.

KNIGHTON (Isle of Wight)

At one time Knighton Gorges was one of the grandest houses on the Isle of Wight. A vast Elizabethan mansion replacing a Norman hall, it was an imposing structure, built onto a crag overlooking the surrounding countryside. It got its name from medieval owners the de Gorges family. Unfortunately, the entire building was torn down in the early 19th century.

Knighton Gorges was an infamously haunted house. Once a year it would be visited by 'the Black Knight', a truly Gothic apparition whom tradition stated had been cursed by a sorcerer to revisit the Earth for evermore. Peter Underwood describes him well, as 'a tall figure in medieval costume, elegant in cape billowing behind him as he gallops his black steed over the quiet and lonely meadows and, when he reaches the lanes and roadways, the pounding hooves echo in the silent, moonlit night…'

Dating from the 18th century is the ghost of a former owner, Sir Tristram Dillington. Dillington suffered an appalling tragedy in 1721, when his wife and all his children died from a fever over the course of one terrible fortnight. He never recovered from the shock and fell into a fit of despair, which ended in him taking his own life not long after. His faithful butler succeeded in making the death look like an accident rather than suicide before alerting the authorities. In those days the estate of a suicide would pass to the Crown rather than his family, and this would have left two unmarried sisters penniless (the butler was later rewarded for his quick thinking with the gift of his own farm). The unhappy spirit of Sir Tristram continued to linger in the house and grounds for years afterwards.

Further ghosts were reported from Knighton Gorges and its vicinity: a phantom carriage charged up the drive; a headless horseman galloped round the encircling lanes; heart-rending sobs sounded from one room, bloodcurdling shrieks from another. In the years following the house's demolition, the strains of sweet and melodious music could sometimes be heard emanating from its former location.

Now we come to the strangest and most current phenomenon reported from Knighton Gorges. The *haunted* house has become a *haunting* house. A number of people, including Ethel Hargrove, author of *England's Garden Island* (published in 1926), claim to have seen Knighton Gorges restored to its former glory, bursting with supernatural life. Miss Hargrove wrote of hearing ghostly music and of seeing the walls and roofs whole and complete, the windows ablaze with light. She and her companion also heard the sounds of revelry, the barking of dogs and then a single gunshot, immediately followed by a rattling of a coach down the former drive. Then all went dark.

In 1915, one man, on a walking tour of the island, claimed to have called at the house, unaware that he was visiting somewhere that had not existed for a century. He had just escaped being run down by a coach in the lane and stomped up to Knighton Gorges, keen to take the driver to task. He knocked repeatedly at the door but no one answered. Peering in through a window, he saw that everyone was wearing Georgian costumes. He wasn't surprised by the sight because it was New Year's Eve and he assumed a fancy dress party was being held. Giving his complaint up as a bad job, he made his way to the nearest inn and told his story there. Trying to identify the house on the map, he could only agree with the locals that his adventure had taken place at 'the site of Knighton Gorges'.

Now it is said that the ghost of Knighton Gorges manifests every New Year's Eve and many claim to have seen the apparition of the house.

NETLEY

The ruins of Netley Abbey date from the 13th century. The abbey was an offshoot of the larger Cistercian house at Beaulieu (see above), much smaller but celebrated for its elegant architecture. After the Dissolution of the Monasteries, it was converted into a private house but by the 18th century the property was in such a state of disrepair that it was sold to a builder who intended to knock it down and recycle the stone for other projects. On the first day of its proposed demolition, however, a chunk of masonry dislodged from the tracery of a particularly beautiful window and, crashing to the ground, killed the builder. Taking this for divine retribution, the wrecking crew threw down their tools and quit the site with alacrity.

Another splendidly Gothic yarn is told about Netley Abbey. A phantom monk had long been known to haunt the ruins and rumour had it he was guarding a valuable treasure, hidden during the Dissolution. During the abbey's period as a private home, a gardener by the name of Slown was working in the grounds one day when he noticed some subsidence. The collapsed soil revealed the entrance to a tunnel. Excited that he may have found the hiding place of the legendary treasure, he dug away until he had excavated a hole big enough for him to enter. His staff waited with bated breath as Slown crawled into the tunnel. Moments later, he came scrabbling out again.

A strange story is told about a window at Netley Abbey, but it is not the strangest tale told about this ruined monastery. Shutterstock/Paul Cummings

Crazed with terror, he began to hurl lumps of mud back into the hole.

'Block it up! For God's sake, block it up!' he screamed.

Slown suffered a nervous collapse and would never reveal what he had seen in the hole. No one else was brave enough to investigate for themselves. Perhaps it was something like the horrible thing David Scanlan and other ghost-hunters saw one night in the Chapterhouse in 2002. In his book, *Paranormal Hampshire*, Scanlan recounts how they noticed what appeared to be 'a large Hessian cloth with something wriggling underneath'. The apparition was only visible in the moonlight: as soon as they switched on their torches, it vanished.

'I remember watching it intently and then something emerged out of the cloth,' Scanlan recalls. 'To be honest, it was horrific. Large bulbous head, large skewer-like teeth, oval eyes and extremely thin.' The thing stretched out an arm, which seemed to grow and grow. The investigators staggered back, and the apparition vanished.

Almost all that survives of the Royal Victoria Military Hospital at Netley is its rather dainty brick chapel. Queen Victoria laid the foundation stone on May 19, 1856, and it was soon caring for up to a thousand injured servicemen at a time (twice that number during the Second World War). Despite its long service, the Military Hospital came in for a considerable amount of criticism, most notably from Florence Nightingale, who considered it 'difficult, depressing and unsatisfactory'. It was so 'depressing' that, according to tradition, a nursing contemporary of Nightingale threw herself to her death from an upper-storey window.

The elegant chapel on the former Victoria Hospital site, Netley, where the 'Lady in Grey' has sometimes been seen. iStock

Ever since, the ghost of the suicide haunted the hospital. She was seen by numerous witnesses, including doctors and clergymen, patrolling the same length of corridor. Because of her old-fashioned nurses' uniform, she was often referred to as the 'Lady in Grey'. Her frequent appearances were hushed up for years, because staff noticed that they invariably preceded a death at the hospital, and they didn't want the patients to become alarmed.

When the hospital was being demolished in 1966, the ghostly nurse became even more active. Freed, it would seem, from the one corridor where she had formerly been confined, the nurse began to be seen in various places, including a passageway leading towards the chapel. Still attached to the place, the chapel is now the only part of the former hospital complex the nurse considers worth haunting. However, she is now not seen nearly as often as she once was.

NEW FOREST

The New Forest covers a large portion of western Hampshire, extending into Wiltshire and Dorset. The original meaning of the word 'forest' is an area of country set aside for hunting. This is often woodland – hence its modern usage – but can also be open country. The New Forest has been 'new' since as long ago as the reign of William the Conqueror, who preserved what was left of the ancient woodland in the area and cleared the heaths of farms and cottages to create a vast area for sport, in particular the hunting of deer. Most of the area is now a National Park.

Despite its name, a number of towns and villages now lie within the boundaries of the New Forest, and a few of these feature in this book. However, I have included this separate entry for ghosts found among the wilder parts of the woods and heaths. The best known of these is a royal ghost.

King William II was the third son of the Conqueror and ruled England from 1087 to 1100. He was known as 'William Rufus' because of his red hair. William met his death in the New Forest in a hunting accident. At least it was presumed to be an accident, but there is some mystery about the incident. The king had been hunting with his younger brother Henry and a group of nobles, including Sir Walter Tyrell. Catching sight of a running stag, Tyrell let fly an arrow, but it glanced off its side and ricocheted into a thicket. Tyrell went to retrieve his arrow and was horrified to discover within the bushes the body of the king – with an arrow embedded in his chest.

Hearing the soon-to-be King Henry and the rest of the party approaching, Tyrell panicked and fled the scene, terrified that they would think he had killed William deliberately. Safely on the other side of the Channel, Tyrell considered the incident more carefully and realised his deflected arrow wouldn't have had enough force to pierce the king's body. Furthermore, he wondered, what had happened to the huntsman who was supposed to accompany the king at all times? The answer to that question, unbeknownst to the worried knight, is that the huntsman had come forward shortly after the discovery of the king's body and firmly put the blame on Tyrell. He had seen him shoot the arrow with calm deliberation, he claimed.

So, who did kill the king? Tyrell? The huntsman? Or was it a deliberate assassination engineered by the king's brother, Henry? Henry was crowned king with almost indecent haste after the death of William, taking advantage, as it seemed, of the absence of the elder brother, Robert, who was away fighting in the Crusades. A more recent theory has it that the assassination was down to an ancient pagan custom in which unworthy kings are ritually killed off. There is not a great deal of credence placed in that idea, though.

Whatever the truth of the sudden death of King William II, ever afterwards his troubled ghost is said to have haunted the place where he fell. The precise spot is marked by a monument known as the Rufus Stone and can be found in Stricknage Wood in the heart of the New Forest. The apparition, which you might encounter near the Rufus Stone on summer evenings, is described as being of a stocky man with red hair and wearing a golden tunic. The ghost wanders about in gloomy contemplation, perhaps still pondering on his death and the reason for it more than 900 years on.

The spectral form of the alleged regicide, Sir Walter Tyrell, also haunts the New Forest. Tyrell's Lane is claimed as the route taken by the knight when he fled the scene. The re-enactment of his headlong flight is said to still take place, a ghostly knight galloping furiously but silently down the lane.

King William II meets his untimely and still mysterious end in the heart of the New Forest. iStock

Other ghosts on horseback have also been encountered in the New Forest. A phantom highwayman, for example, haunts a heath at Durhurst Cross, and another horseman still rides past the tree at Durley Lawn, from which he was hanged in 1759. The apparition of Sir William de Vernon – one of the knights who forced Bad King John to sign the Magna Carta – rides up to the isolated church at Boldre, then, dismounting, marches up to the altar, kneels before it and vanishes. He is accompanied by an equally ghostly pair of archers. Sir William held the estate of Boldre in the 13th century.

The lovely old church at Breamore is haunted by monks, thought to be the spirits of those whose stone coffins were dug up on the neighbouring site of an old priory and deposited in the graveyard. The nearby 'mizmaze', a maze of low-cut turf, may date back to prehistoric times. The monks at the aforementioned priory used the maze in a novel way: they forced repentant sinners to creep along it on their knees while offering up prayers for forgiveness. Muffled moans and shuffles are still said to emanate from the mizmaze.

Across the way is Breamore House, now home to an agricultural museum. It is haunted by elder and younger female members of the Dodington family. They are each distinctly melancholy ghosts, bringing misfortune to those unlucky enough to see them, and a painting of the elder Mrs Dodington in mourning dress is said to be cursed: injury or death is bound to befall anyone foolish enough to move or otherwise interfere with it.

A most affecting ghost haunts Thorney Hill, near Burley. This is the spectre of a small boy, a miserable wraith in threadbare clothes, who runs down a track leading to Picket Post, sobbing pitifully. The desperately sad story told to explain his presence is that he was drowned in a well centuries ago by parents who couldn't afford to feed him.

The New Forest is well known for the near-wild horses that roam its fields and heaths. According to Anthony Brode's *Haunted Hampshire*, there is one place they will not stray: a small area of Hazeley Heath. Numerous people have said they have observed horses suddenly shy away from this patch and have felt an uneasy atmosphere there themselves. Tradition has it a fierce battle was fought on this spot during the Roman occupation and that the animals in particular are sensitive to the ensuing psychic residue.

Horses roaming the New Forest. A number of ghosts wander the wilder parts of the New Forest and in at least one place the horses are nervously aware of them. iStock

Donkeys are also a feature of the New Forest landscape, often stubbornly blocking traffic by ambling along or lying down in the middle of the narrow roads. At least one of them is said to be a ghost: a 'ghastly white' creature that haunts the Forest near the border with Wiltshire.

ODIHAM

Just one chunk of Odiham Castle survives, a decidedly weathered ruin but well worth a visit for its attractive, secluded situation. A major renovation project by Hampshire County Council has recently (2014) been completed at the castle. Its present state belies its former importance. It was built on the command of King John and remained one of his favourite residences. It was from Odiham Castle that John rode out to Runnymede to sign the Magna Carta.

Its best-known ghost is an unusual one: a medieval minstrel. It is more often heard than seen, a voice raised in a – literally – haunting old song, accompanied by the strains of a lute. Those who say they've seen him describe the minstrel as wearing the traditional outfit of patchwork of many colours. Weird, shadowy shapes have also been reported moving about within the crumbling masonry. These may be the sad spectres of former prisoners.

In the attractive olde worlde village itself, a number of other ghosts have been recorded. One of these is a suitably traditional phantom: a Black Dog that runs through its High Street and then out into the surrounding countryside after dark. Peter Underwood, who was himself a Hampshire resident, was told of a spectral coachman who had stepped out in front of a car on the Farnham Road just outside Odiham. The witness described the figure as wearing 'a long, old-fashioned coat … three-cornered hat, gaiters and shoes with big brass buckles'. He also carried a whip, which identified his occupation. The driver had pulled over and wound down the window, assuming that this oddly dressed man had needed a lift. The ghost seemed to be asking something like 'Has the coachman left the turnpike?' and then it vanished.

The unusual ghost of Odiham Castle dates from its medieval heyday.
Shutterstock/BasPhoto

PORTCHESTER

The mighty fortress of Portchester Castle stands guard over the northern end of Portsmouth Harbour. It started life as a Roman fort and still has the highest standing Roman walls in Europe. A succession of medieval kings increased Portchester's size and importance over the centuries. It served as a base for a number of warmongering expeditions to France, including Edward III's campaign which saw success at Crécy in 1346 and Henry V's campaign which culminated in victory at Agincourt in 1415.

Ironically, it became the home of the daughter of the King of France, Isabella, after she married Richard II at the tender age of seven. In the 18th century it served as a prison for more subjects of France during the Napoleonic Wars. Thereafter it was allowed to fall into disrepair but the ruins (in the care of English Heritage) are still impressive.

There was a priory within the castle grounds and this would probably explain the ghostly form of a monk in a brown habit which walks here. It makes its way past the castle frontage, slowly fading away with every step. A church dating from the 12th century is also found on site and this is haunted by a woman with long dark hair and a sorrowful expression. There is also a long-standing tradition of a tall figure in white haunting Portchester Castle, but one source states that a half-forgotten prank carried out in 1900 is responsible for this account.

The massive ruins of Portchester Castle are haunted by a number of ghosts. iStock

PORTSMOUTH

This historic naval port boasts the world's oldest dry dock and is home to several famous ships, including Henry VIII's *Mary Rose* and Nelson's HMS *Victory*. It is still a busy port today and the city – the only one in the UK on an island – is Hampshire's second largest.

In the 19th century a naval officer by the name of Hamilton had a spooky experience in Portsmouth. He had arrived in the town to rejoin his ship but it was late in arriving, so he had to put up for the night. Due to a number of factors, including an election being held in the town, accommodation was hard to come by but Mr Hamilton found a pub that would take him in. It was called the Admiral Collingwood. The landlady told him she only had a twin-bedded room available but Hamilton paid for both beds so that he could have the room to himself. In the middle of the night, however, he awoke to find the other bed was occupied: the outline of a man was clear under the bedclothes. Hamilton was annoyed at this intrusion, considering how much he had paid for the room, but he was tired and decided to leave any row until the morning. He rolled over and settled back to sleep.

The following morning the man was still present in the next bed. Hamilton was puzzled as well as irritated because he now remembered that he had locked the door before retiring for the night. He slipped out of bed and crossed the room. He saw that the stranger was a young sailor with dark hair and a beard. Across his temple there was a wound, the blood from which had apparently still been flowing when the sailor had gone to bed, for it had stained the pillow beneath his head. Detecting no sound of breathing, Hamilton felt some concern and reached out to gently wake the stranger. As he did so, the man vanished. The bed returned to its pristine, unslept-in condition.

The shaken Hamilton now accosted the landlady, who assured him that no one else had had use of the room beside himself. When Hamilton described the man to her, however, she became distraught. She admitted that a few weeks previously three sailors had occupied the room and a violent altercation had broken out between them. One of the men – who had sported dark whiskers like those Hamilton had described – received a fatal blow on the side of the head. The other two men threatened the landlady, convincing her to allow them to bury their dead comrade in her garden. As well as fearing for

'The Arrival of the Fleet', an 18th-century cartoon depicting rowdy behaviour in Portsmouth Harbour. The city has a number of haunted locations and many are linked with its maritime history.

her own safety, she had been worried about the reputation of her inn, and so had reluctantly agreed.

Years later Hamilton returned to Portsmouth but was unable to find the Admiral Collingwood. As far as he could tell, it had been converted into a shop.

The White Swan Inn in Guildhall Walk is allegedly haunted by a murdered barmaid. Legend has it the young woman's husband was a sailor and that while he was away at sea her affections strayed – more than once. On one of the sailor's shore leaves, he found out about his wife's infidelities. Enraged with jealousy, he lashed out at the barmaid with his splicing knife, killing her where she stood by the pub's grand fireplace. The girl's ghost is said to still haunt the vicinity of the fireplace.

One of Portsmouth's better known haunted buildings, the New Theatre Royal, is also situated in Guildhall Walk. Despite its 'New' appellation, the theatre is a grand old dame dating from the 1850s. The New Theatre Royal is haunted by its first manager, Henry Rutley, and by an actor who slit his own throat in a dressing room in the 1880s or 1890s (sources vary). Spooky incidents have since been reported from it, including disembodied footsteps, lights that switch themselves on and off at will, and eerie 'whisperings and sighs'.

Many of the places linked to Portsmouth's illustrious naval past are haunted. Fort Cumberland in Southsea is now in the care of English Heritage. Its ghost is of a spy of the Napoleonic period who was apprehended and hanged in the fort. His spirit has been heard pacing about, up and down a staircase to a room where, last century, a mysterious fire once broke out – possibly caused by the ghost.

The equally restless spirits of Napoleonic Prisoners of War are said to haunt Fort Widley, on Portsdown Hill, along with a phantom drummer boy. The ghost of a little girl, a naval officer's daughter who accidentally fell to her death from one of the ramparts, has been seen at nearby Fort Purbrook. Fort Nelson, which now houses the Royal Armouries Museum, is haunted by a sentry who was found drunk on duty and confined to the cells pending a court martial. In shame and remorse, he took his own life. The cells can now be visited and many tourists have reported feeling a sensation of dread here.

Portsmouth Harbour is haunted by a man who was executed for starting a fire in the rope house of the naval dockyard. His body was hung in chains on Blockhouse Point and it is said the rattling of his chains can still be heard – a traditional form of haunting rarely found outside Gothic fiction.

Of all the places in Portsmouth where paranormal activity has been reported, the most celebrated must surely be HMS *Victory*. The *Victory* was Lord Nelson's flagship at the Battle of Trafalgar in 1805. Nelson died during the battle, after a musket ball penetrated his shoulder and lodged in his spine. HMS *Victory*, a 104-gunner, was launched in 1765 and after centuries of active service was berthed in Portsmouth's dry dock in the 1920s, where she has been preserved as a museum ship. However, she remains the flagship of the First Sea Lord and is the oldest ship of the line still in commission. Today the *Victory*, restored to a state Nelson would have recognised, is open to the public and can be explored to gain a real insight

Inexplicable activity has been reported aboard Nelson's flagship, HMS Victory.
iStock

into life above and below decks in the days when Britain ruled the waves.

Over the years there have been claims of 'unearthly sounds' being heard on board and of glimpses of 'mysterious fleeting figures' around the ship. David Scanlan spoke to a naval rating who told him that he and other members of the security team aboard the *Victory* had, on more than one occasion, found huge barrels had moved about overnight. The barrels are solidly made replicas of those that would originally have stored provisions and it takes two or three people to move them. It was a complete mystery as to how they could find their way up a flight of steps when no one had been around to shift them.

RINGWOOD

Moyles Court is now used by a private school but in the 17th century it was the home of an indomitable old lady by the name of Dame Alice Lisle. In 1685 Dame Alice found herself caught up in the Monmouth Rebellion. The First Duke of Monmouth, an illegitimate son of Charles II, raised a force in the West of England to try and claim the throne in place of his uncle, James II. Monmouth hoped that the fact that he was a Protestant would find favour with those who disapproved of the Catholicism of James II. But the rebellion was quashed at the Battle of Sedgemoor and the ruthless 'Hanging' Judge Jeffreys was put in charge of prosecuting surviving rebels.

Jeffreys was under orders to make sure no such rebellion would occur again, and his response was merciless: hanging hundreds of people for treason, many of whom may have had nothing to do with the uprising. One of those he caught in his net was

Alice Lisle. Dame Alice had had no part or even sympathy with the Rebellion but had taken pity on two men who had been on the losing side and who had fled the scene. Moyles Court was searched and the fugitives were found sheltering there. Even though they had not yet been found guilty of treason, Jeffreys considered the harbouring of them to be treason anyway. And treason carried a death sentence. Dame Alice was taken to Winchester to be executed and was there beheaded, despite considerable protest.

Ever since this injustice, the ghost of Dame Alice Lisle is said to have returned to Moyles Court and the lanes round about it. Some say she is seen with her head poignantly – and traditionally – tucked underneath her arm; others that she rides up to the manor house in a spectral carriage drawn by headless horses. The strong scent of violets has been detected at unexpected times in Moyles Court and it is thought that this too might be an indication of Dame Alice's ghostly presence, although there is no evidence that this was an especially favoured perfume of hers. As well as Moyles Court, Dame Alice is said to have haunted a house owned by her son at Dibden, fifteen miles away, and the Eclipse Inn at Winchester (see the section on Winchester below).

ROMSEY

The violent upheavals of the English Civil War have placed their psychic mark on the British Isles more than any other period in history. An astonishing number of ghosts date from the few years the war played out. One of the many horror stories told about the conflict occurred in the Market Place in Romsey.

A party of Royalists made use of the wrought iron bracket supporting the old Swan Inn's sign to hang two Roundhead soldiers they had captured. However, one of them did not expire as he was suspended from the bracket. He managed to free himself and tried to make his escape through the market. Alas, he did not get far before he was cut down by his captors. He died in a spot where, subsequently, a row of Georgian shops were built. In one of the buildings (formerly the Palmerston restaurant), the unhappy spirit of the twice-murdered soldier made his presence known by treading the upper floors with invisible feet, shoving people in the back with invisible hands and opening and closing doors in an eerie manner. He has even been known to flush the toilet when 'the littlest room' is otherwise empty of occupants.

Just off the square is the White Horse Hotel, whose Georgian facade belies a medieval origin. An anonymous White Lady patrols the so-called Mummers Gallery in the hotel, peering down on passers-by. Another phantom woman dressed in white haunts the former Corn Exchange, now a store, in the town centre. Her origin is likewise unknown. Sometimes this latter ghost is seen wearing a blue dress.

SHANKLIN (Isle of Wight)

Vernon Cottage in Shanklin Old Village is now a restaurant but was originally a private home. It is named after an Admiral Vernon, a fiery individual who was always chafing at the bit during times of peace. In 1739, despite an uneasy truce existing between Spain and Great Britain, Vernon convinced the Admiralty to let him take a squadron of just six ships to capture the Spanish port of Porto Bello in Panama. He succeeded, with the loss of just three men.

The ghost of Vernon Cottage could not be more different from this indomitable old sea-dog, however. It is of a young girl, who is seen in broad daylight running from the restaurant and down the lane, where she meets the apparition of a young man before vanishing. The reason for the haunting is unknown. Was this her last meeting with a boyfriend who proved treacherous, maybe even murderous? Let us hope not. Let us hope instead that the little scenario still played out is a rare example of extreme joy rather than misery or tragedy creating a psychic impression.

Shanklin's famous Pier Theatre was destroyed, along with the pier itself, by a great storm in 1987. For many years it was apparently haunted by a Victorian entertainer by the name of Albert DuBois (not to be confused with the French painter). He was a distinctive figure: tall, with impressive whiskers and a diamond-studded cravat. His phantom was spotted on a number of occasions in various parts of the theatre. In addition disembodied footsteps were heard thumping up a short flight of steps leading to the stage, and unearthly cold spots were encountered in a number of places. One seat in the auditorium was particularly prone to this uncomfortable chill – had DuBois set this seat aside for his own particular use?

Shanklin Old Village, where the apparition of a girl has been seen running to meet her equally ghostly boyfriend. iStock

SOUTHAMPTON

Southampton is the largest city in Hampshire but has only a few haunted locations. However, these do include some attractive old properties, including two medieval pubs. The Red Lion, in the High Street, is a largely Tudor building with a Victorian frontage but the earliest parts of the building date back to the 13th century, when it was used as a courthouse. An extraordinary trial took place here during the reign of King Henry V.

Henry V is remembered today as a heroic king, this image being mainly due to Shakespeare's portrayal of him. However, at the start of his reign he was not universally popular. His father, Henry IV, was a usurper, who had taken the throne from the ineffectual Richard II. By the time Henry V took the throne, Richard's legitimate heir, his nephew the Earl of March, was an adult and was proving himself to be a much more capable man than his uncle had been. There were those who wanted to see March on the throne, rather than Henry (although the sensible earl did not share this ambition himself). The conspirators decided to murder Henry at Southampton, so that March would inevitably become king, whatever personal views he may have had on the subject.

The plot was exposed, however, by Sir John Oldcastle (who some believe may have been the model for Shakespeare's Falstaff). Although Oldcastle had had well-publicised disagreements with Henry, he did not support treason and the conspirators made a poor choice in seeking to include him in their circle. The plotters were arrested and a trial was held in what is now the Red Lion. Three ringleaders were found guilty of treason: Lord Henry Scrope, Richard, Earl of Cambridge, and Sir Thomas Grey. They were immediately marched out to the Bargate, part of Southampton's original city walls (which still survives), and there beheaded for their crime.

The ghosts of the three conspirators are now said to haunt the Red Lion. With bowed heads and wearing the fancy outfits one would expect to grace the forms of medieval noblemen, they emerge from the front door and shuffle off in the direction of the Bargate.

Elsewhere in the High Street can be found the Dolphin Hotel, which, despite its smart Georgian exterior, is actually older than the Red Lion: it dates back to the 1100s. When Rupert

SOUTHAMPTON, FROM THE PIER.

*Southampton in the 19th century. The city's ghosts include medieval noblemen,
18th-century dandies, Victorian chambermaids and (possibly) Anne Boleyn.*
iStock

Matthews visited the Dolphin, he was shown over the haunted parts of the hotel by the landlord. These included the medieval cellars, which are haunted by a young boy and an older man. The boy's identity is a mystery but the man is thought to be 'Tom', a cellarman who looked after the barrels of wine more than a century ago.

More frequently seen is 'Molly', who haunts an area of the ground floor that was rebuilt in the 1890s after a fire. In life Molly was a chambermaid who, spurned by her lover, hanged herself in a stable block. The stable appears to have been replaced by the Victorian rooms. One witness who saw Molly said that only the top half of her was visible, possibly because the floor level of the stable was lower than that of the rooms which replaced it.

On the first floor can be found the 18th-century Assembly Rooms, which formerly hosted the cream of Georgian and Regency society (including a young Jane Austen, who danced here on her 18th birthday). The splendidly attired ghost of a Georgian dandy, nicknamed 'Beau' by staff, has been witnessed standing in one of the bay windows. He gazes out rather forlornly, as if looking out for the arrival of someone whom he has all but given up on. His rather ample figure has also been seen from the street below, peering down from the same window.

Another haunted historical property in Southampton is the Tudor House Museum in the Old Town. The impressive black-and-white building gets its name from the extensive rebuilding work carried out in the early 16th century by a former owner, Sir John Dawtrey, whose jobs at the time included the fitting out of the *Mary Rose* and other ships in King Henry VIII's navy. However, the house dates back to the 12th century and is considered one of the finest examples of Norman domestic architecture in England.

'Dark figures' have been glimpsed around the Tudor House, and other phenomena, including odd scraping noises, mysterious footsteps and the inexplicable ringing of a bell, have been reported. For some reason dogs absolutely refuse to enter the Green Room, as if they are aware of a presence undetectable by humans. Between the years 1545 to 1552 the Tudor House was home to the Lord Chief Justice of England, Sir Richard Lyster. During his residency the house was visited by Henry VIII and one of his ill-fated queens, Anne Boleyn. The apparition of a woman in Tudor costume is thought, perhaps rather optimistically, to be of Anne.

A pitiful procession of ghosts which makes its way to Southampton's Bargate recalls an execution which took place during the reign of Henry V. iStock

The Medieval Merchant's House on French Street is another rare survivor and is also open to the public. It was built in 1290 for a wine merchant, John Fortin, who kept his imported goods at a nice, constant temperature in the undercroft. It is the only example of a building of this type and period to survive substantially as originally built. When the Luftwaffe bombed Southampton in 1940, destroying most of the front end of French Street, the building escaped destruction, but what damage it did sustain revealed its medieval interior. It was restored and later given over to the care of English Heritage.

Prior to the house becoming a museum, the residents said that they were repeatedly visited by the ghost of a young woman who stood silently at the foot of the bed. They also reported doors opening and closing by themselves and other odd goings-on. In the 1950s, the Student Players, an amateur dramatic society, made use of the Medieval Merchant's House. Members of the group reported a range of strange phenomena during their time there, including the sound of disembodied footsteps on the stairs and an unpleasant sensation of being pushed from behind when walking along the landing.

One of the Players was a medium – or at least so she told the others – and she suggested a séance to get to the bottom of the apparent haunting. Those with her at the time agreed, and an impromptu séance was organised. The name 'Ruth Dill' came through on the Ouija board and they learnt that while the building was being used as a boarding house many years ago, Ruth had murdered a sailor staying in the house for the jewels he had carried back from foreign parts. Ruth had then hidden the gems in a well and it was her unhappy spirit which haunted the house. One of the group scoffed at the revelation, saying it was all made up, whereupon the heavy oak table they were sitting round lifted from the ground and hurled itself across the room!

A search for the well – hopefully with the jewels still hidden in it – proved fruitless, however. Indeed no well has ever been discovered, although it seems reasonable that one must have existed at one time. In 1963 another séance was held, this time by a self-publicising medium named Sybil Leek, and the BBC were called in to film it. One of those present was Anthony Brode, who writes about it in his own book on *Haunted Hampshire*. The results were inconclusive but the BBC cameramen were impressed by the sight of a table rising up on one leg while the planchette was in operation and then 'walking' round the room while the sitters held on (this was a deal card-table and not the heavy oak table used previously).

The Medieval Merchant's House in Southampton is believed to be haunted by a murderess. iStock

TOTTON

Totton is a small town on the southern edge of suburban Southampton. Now used as offices, Testwood House has long had a reputation for paranormal activity. The apparition of a man wearing a long coat and a tall hat has been encountered both inside and outside the house. Most often he has been seen on the drive walking to the front door or at the front door itself.

On one occasion, the face of a young man with a melancholy expression and grey eyes was seen staring out of the window of a room that was immediately afterwards found to be empty and which had been securely locked. On another, an employee in the building saw a mysterious man apparently sitting on the other side of the desk in reception. He had his back to the observer and appeared to be laughing, though silently. The witness felt an unearthly chill descend on him and he hurried out in a strange sort of panic. In addition to the male ghosts (which may perhaps be all of the same man), a female phantom has been seen in an attic bedroom.

Legend has it that a century or more ago a coachman murdered the cook at Testwood House, then dragged her body down the drive and over the road before dumping her in a lane still called Cooks Lane to this day. The ghosts may well relate to this tragedy and so too might the spectral coach which rattles up the drive and the sound of heavy masculine footsteps treading down an empty corridor.

VENTNOR (Isle of Wight)

Ventnor was one of Victorian England's favourite watering places. The town, which was developed in a sheltered spot beneath a cliff, is noticeably warmer and sunnier than most places in the British Isles. The warmth and sunshine was not only appreciated by tourists. Combined with the supposed health-giving properties of sea air, these properties highlighted Ventnor as an ideal location for a hospital specialising in the care of people with breathing difficulties and diseases of the lungs.

Consumption – today called tuberculosis – was one of the 19th century's biggest killers. At that time it was incurable, but an escape from the polluted air of the cities was one way to help ease its symptoms. The Royal National Hospital for Diseases of the Chest was founded in 1869 and soon became the centre of excellence in the treatment on tuberculosis. In 1964, it was closed down and in 1969 it was demolished, exactly a century after it was founded. By this time tuberculosis had become a curable disease.

During the demolition of the hospital, workers on the site reported a range of spooky incidents. Eerie groans and sighs would be heard about the site. Machinery would constantly break down and electrics act up. Then the phantom of a little girl began to be glimpsed by the men.

After the demolition process was complete, the location had a wonderful transformation. Making the most of the sunny, sheltered microclimate, the Ventnor Botanic Garden was established. The temperatures here are more like the Mediterranean than the UK and frost is a rare occurrence, allowing a wide range of temperate and sub-tropical plants and shrubs to be grown that would struggle elsewhere. In this tranquil environment, however, the ghosts of the past are still said to manifest. Apparitions of former patients at the hospital are still occasionally to be encountered wandering along the paths between the flower beds.

Another spooky occurrence took place in a Ventnor garden some years ago. As Peter Underwood outlines the incident, a gardener was planting shrubs at a house named Craigie Lodge when he turned up the jawbone of a child. Further digging revealed an entire skeleton.

Staying at the house at the time was a psychic by the name of Mrs Pollock. Mrs Pollock claimed to have the power of

The Esplanade at Ventnor. The town's mild climate attracted invalids,
some of whom seem to have found it so pleasant that they continue to linger here.
Shutterstock/Dave Turner

psychometry, the ability to pick up psychic vibrations through objects. She took up one of the child's bones and placed it against her forehead. She then announced that she felt sure another skeleton was waiting to be found close by. She was right: the remains of a woman were soon unearthed beside those of the child. Unfortunately, Mrs Pollock's powers were insufficient to shed light on the identities of the bodies or the reason why they lay in unmarked graves in the garden of Craigie Lodge. Those mysteries have remained unsolved.

WATERLOOVILLE

According to tradition, Waterlooville is named after a pub, the Heroes of Waterloo, which opened in 1815, just in time to welcome sailors returning victorious from the Battle of Waterloo. The pub stood at the crossroads in the centre of town, near where the much more recent pub of the same name now stands.

Waterlooville is home to a property which used to have a decidedly sinister reputation: Hopfield House, in Maralyn Avenue. A Gothic revival house of the early Victorian period, Hopfield was built by an austere gentleman by the name of Edward Fawkes. Fawkes saw the house as his lifetime's achievement and he was obsessed with the idea that it should remain the Fawkes family home forever. As it transpired, though, the family decided to move out of the house just two generations later. They transferred themselves to Southsea and rented Hopfield House to a retired naval officer and his wife. It is from this point that Hopfield's sinister reputation begins.

Soon after moving in, the new tenant telephoned to say that he had just been visited by the angry spirit of Edward Fawkes. The ghost told him he had no right to live in the house and he wanted them to quit it forthwith. Dire consequences would befall any 'strangers' at Hopfield. This astonishing communication wasn't taken at all seriously by the owners but in time they came to realise the naval officer was in earnest. In the coming weeks he was to tell them of repeated visits by Fawkes's spectre, and he urged them to allow him to sub-let to someone else, so that he and his wife could move elsewhere. This was reluctantly agreed.

Unfortunately, things didn't improve. A widowed woman and her daughter moved in but, within a few months, the older of them was found dead. As far as was known, she had been in good health. The distraught daughter begged to be able to give up the tenancy and this was agreed. The family couldn't help but wonder whether the tale of their ancestor's vengeful ghost didn't have some truth in it after all. They decided to sell Hopfield House.

But things got worse. The new owner, a recently retired captain, was found in the hallway with one of his collection of ornamental daggers sticking out of his back. The murderer was never caught and the widow promptly left. Once again Hopfield was sold, this time to the Nowells. The Nowells set about improving the house, softening its rather gaunt exterior, and adding all-new 'mod cons' (we are now into the 1920s). It is from the daughter of the house at that time, Sheila Nowells, that we learn of the hauntings.

Sheila experienced a bizarre but frightening night soon after moving in. She was awoken by the sound of her pet dog growling ferociously – and discovered that she was now lying under her bed rather than in it. She had somehow been transported beneath it as she slept. She struggled out to see her dog snarling at the bedroom door, which was slowly opening. Sheila stared in a state of horrified suspense. The door opened wide to reveal – no one.

Sheila's bedroom door continued to open by itself for nights on end. Although this was the only strange phenomenon to be observed in Hopfield during the Nowells' time here, it continued to be a cursed house. Sheila's brother shot himself in the cellar for reasons that never became known. The shock led to her mother's early death and her father collapsed and died a few months after Mrs Nowells passed away. Sheila never returned to Hopfield House again. It has long since been converted into flats but, so far as is known, no further visits from Edward Fawkes or other ghostly or ghastly incidents have occurred there in recent times.

WINCHESTER

The ancient city of Winchester is also Hampshire's county town. England's first king, Edgar, was crowned here and Alfred the Great made it his capital. Some consider Winchester the first capital of England before the seat of power was shifted to London. There is much to be found in the city of antiquarian interest, including its impressive cathedral, one of the best-preserved medieval guild halls in the country (home to a 13th-century replica of King Arthur's Round Table), and Winchester College, one of England's oldest schools.

Winchester Cathedral is one of the biggest in Britain; indeed it has a greater length than any in Europe. Construction began shortly after the Norman Conquest to replace the Saxon church (known as the Old Minster) which was situated nearby. Much of the interior is solid Norman architecture, with Gothic additions and a beautiful crypt augmented in 1986 with a soulful statue by Antony Gormley.

Spectral monks have been reported from Winchester Cathedral. According to Peter Underwood, one of the hooded figures walks down the aisle and then, rather disconcertingly, climbs up non-existent steps, before disappearing. The other, state Rupert Matthews and David Scanlan, is seen in the cathedral close and has a noticeable limp. It makes its painful but silent way from the southern end of the close to the arch, where it melts away.

Spooky photographs have also been taken at Winchester Cathedral. In 1957 a tourist took a photo which appeared to show thirteen ghostly figures kneeling down before the altar. The photographer was adamant that no one was at prayer in front of the altar when he took the picture. A snap taken on a separate occasion shows a figure which has been tentatively identified as a medieval workman.

Phantom monks have been seen in Winchester town centre since as long ago as the 17th century. They are thought to be the ghosts of funeral processions to the monks' burial ground now occupied by a section of George Street. In his *Haunted Hampshire*, Rupert Matthews quotes a man who saw a solitary ghost in nearby Royal Oak Passage. He said the monk was entirely shrouded in his habit, snuggled in as if he was cold, despite the fact that it was a warm summer's evening.

Winchester Cathedral is one of the largest in Britain. It is haunted by two phantom monks. iStock

However, as the monk passed him, he felt an unearthly chill and, on turning round, he was startled to see that the figure had vanished.

Winchester also has two very old and very haunted pubs. The Eclipse Inn, near the cathedral, featured in a dramatic incident which took place in 1685. On September 2 of that year Dame Alice Lisle (see 'Ringwood', above) was beheaded for giving refuge to men who had fought in the Monmouth Rebellion. After her conviction, Dame Alice was held prisoner in an upstairs room of the Eclipse while a scaffold was constructed outside her room. She stepped from her window onto the scaffold and, in the face of considerable injustice, met her cruel fate with dignity.

The ghost of Dame Alice Lisle – described as 'a tall woman in a long grey woollen dress' – has been seen in the room where she was held and in the corridor outside. The sound of 'rough voices' and hammering has also been reported by occupants of the room as being heard at night.

The Hyde Tavern in Hyde Street is claimed to be Winchester's oldest hostelry. The ghost here has not been seen but in previous years made its presence known by yanking the blankets off guests' beds. This odd habit is not uncommonly reported in haunted properties. However, the behaviour at the Hyde is thought to relate specifically to an unpleasant incident which occurred centuries ago. A starving beggar woman was unkindly turned away from the inn and she died later that night of cold and hunger. It is thought her spirit then took up residence in the Hyde Tavern and that she may be removing the clothes from the comfortable beds as a reminder of her cold and lonely last night on Earth.

The Theatre Royal was formerly a hotel. It was converted into a theatre just before the First World War by two brothers, James and John Simpkins. James Simpkins fixed a plaque above the stage displaying the letters 'JS'. It's possible he intended the 'J' to represent the first names of both brothers, but John was offended and asked James to set up a new sign where the ownership was more clear: 'J&JS'. This James

Spooky goings-on take place at a number of properties in Winchester after dark.
iStock

refused to do, and they were still rowing about it when John fell ill and died. Now, it is said, John Simpkins's melancholy-looking ghost wanders the circle, pauses to examine the disputed plaque, and then passes across the stage and through a wall into an area where his old office stood.

WROXALL (Isle of Wight)

Appuldurcombe House was formerly one of the grandest estates on the Isle of Wight. Sadly, the impressive Baroque house was badly damaged by bombing during the Second World War and was subsequently abandoned. Today it is merely a shell but is still worth a visit thanks to its splendid Capability Brown-designed landscaped grounds (Appuldurcombe is looked after by English Heritage).

The ghosts most commonly seen in and around the house are of monks. These are thought to be the shades of Benedictine monks who stayed at Appuldurcombe between 1901 and 1907 after they had been turned out of their former home in France. They later moved on to nearby Quarr Abbey. However, it's possible that one or more of them dates from the Norman priory that was on the site centuries before the house was built.

One rather unpleasant story tells of a monk being locked up in the bowels of Appuldurcombe House by his brothers because they thought he was mad. They would let him out at night, so that he could get some exercise and fresh air when his behaviour would not be likely to disturb their neighbours. They even gave him a hand-bell to ring as he wandered about the lanes and fields, so that anyone who wished to avoid him could do so. In fact, the locals got used to the harmless fellow as he pottered about, dolefully ringing his bell from time to time. It is said his ghost is still sometimes to be encountered on moonlit nights in the lanes round Appuldurcombe House and his bell is still sometimes to be heard clanging over the fields.

Appuldurcombe House is haunted by monks, including one who allegedly went insane. Shutterstock/BasPhoto